SMALL QUOTES, BIG LESSONS

LIFE WISDOM FROM A 6TH GRADER'S HEART

AADYA SINGH

Made with ♥ on the Notion Press Platform
www.notionpress.com

To my parents, for your endless love and guidance,
To my sister, for being my forever friend and cheerleader,
And to my teachers, for inspiring me every day.
Thank you for teaching me life's biggest lessons.

Contents

Foreword

Life teaches us valuable lessons through simple moments. In Small Quotes, Big Lessons, Aadya Singh shares thoughtful words on kindness, friendship, courage, and gratitude—reminding us that wisdom often lies in small gestures.

Enjoy this inspiring collection, and let Aadya's insights brighten your day and encourage you to grow wiser, one quote at a time.

— Chandra Prabha Singh

Preface

This book began as a simple idea—to collect the thoughts, quotes, and lessons that have touched my heart. As I wrote, I realised how much we can learn from everyday moments, from people around us, and from the little things that often go unnoticed.

Small Quotes, Big Lessons is my way of sharing what I've learned so far, in the hope that it brings smiles, thoughts, and warmth to others too.

I'm grateful to my parents, sister, and teachers for always encouraging me to express myself.

I hope you enjoy reading this book as much as I enjoyed creating it.

— Aadya Singh

Grade 6, Section B

Acknowledgements

I would like to thank everyone who helped and supported me in creating this book.

To my parents – thank you for always believing in me and encouraging me to dream big.

To my sister – for your constant cheer and being my best friend.

To my teachers – for inspiring me every day and helping me discover the joy of writing.

This book would not have been possible without your love, support, and guidance.

— Aadya Singh

Prologue

Big lessons often hide in the simplest moments—a kind word, a mistake, a quiet thought. As I began paying attention to these moments in my everyday life, I found myself learning things I wanted to remember and share.

This book is a small collection of those thoughts—quotes and reflections that helped me understand life a little better. They're not perfect or fancy, but they're honest and real.

I hope these pages make you pause, smile, and maybe even see your own experiences in a new light.

— Aadya Singh

CHAPTER ONE

Happiness

1. "Happiness grows when we share it, just like a plant grows when watered."
Lesson: Share your joy with others, and you'll feel even happier.
2. "The best smiles come from the smallest moments."
Lesson: Find joy in small things like a sunny day, a tasty snack, or playing with friends.
3. "If you carry happiness in your pocket, sadness finds no place."
Lesson: Keep positive thoughts close to your heart to stay cheerful.
4. "Happiness isn't a destination—it's a feeling you find on the way."
Lesson: Don't wait to be happy someday; look for joy in the present.
5. "Laughter is the sunshine that helps us grow through cloudy days."
Lesson: Smiling and laughing lightens even the toughest times.

Enter Caption

CHAPTER TWO

Kindness

1. "Kindness is the strongest magic you can perform without a wand."
Lesson: Being kind changes people's days and makes the world better.
2. "Your words can heal or hurt. Choose kindness always."
Lesson: Think before you speak. Words are powerful tools.
3. "Even a small act of kindness ripples through the world like water in a pond."
Lesson: No act of kindness is too small or insignificant.
4. "Kindness costs nothing, but gives everything."
Lesson: Being kind doesn't need effort, but it creates deep impact.
5. "When you choose kindness, you choose courage too."
Lesson: It takes strength to be gentle in a harsh world.

Enter Caption

CHAPTER THREE

Friendship

1. "Friends are like stars; sometimes you can't see them, but you know they're always there."
Lesson: True friends will always support you, even if they're not nearby.
2. "A friend is someone who sees your imperfections as perfectly fine."
Lesson: Real friends accept you exactly as you are.
3. "Friendship doubles your happiness and halves your sadness."
Lesson: Sharing your feelings with friends makes joy bigger and troubles smaller.

CHAPTER FOUR

Courage

1. "Courage doesn't mean never feeling scared. It means taking a step even if you're afraid."
Lesson: Being brave means doing the right thing even when it's tough.
2. "Every brave step forward shrinks your fears a little more."
Lesson: Face your fears; each time you do, you become stronger.
3. "Real courage is being yourself, even if you feel different."
Lesson: Embrace who you are; your uniqueness is your strength.

CHAPTER FIVE

Perseverence

1. "Mistakes are proof that you are trying. Keep going."
Lesson: Don't fear mistakes; they help you learn and grow.
2. "Great things happen when you refuse to give up."
Lesson: Determination turns dreams into reality.
3. "The finish line is closer with each step you take. Don't stop moving."
Lesson: Small steps forward eventually lead you to success.

CHAPTER SIX

Gratitude

1. "Gratitude is noticing little blessings hidden in everyday moments."
   Lesson: Always notice and appreciate good things around you.
2. "Thankfulness makes everything brighter, like sunshine after the rain."
   Lesson: Being grateful makes tough days easier to manage.
3. "If you count your blessings instead of problems, you'll always have reasons to smile."
   Lesson: Focus on positives rather than negatives for a happier life.

Conclusion Life Gives Us Endless Lessons To Learn. Sometimes The Most Important Ones Are Hidden In Simple Words, Quiet Moments, And Daily Actions. Kee